Paradise High

Annie Dalton

Illustrated by David Kearney

OXFORD
UNIVERSITY PRESS

1

Thursdays in Paradise

Every Thursday after school, Karen and I used to race out of the gate at top speed. On other days, ordinary days, we'd giggle and goof about all the way home. But on Thursdays, we were deadly serious, like secret agents on a special mission.

We'd pound along the road in silence, only stopping to buy a bottle of coke. We usually made it back to my house with ten minutes to spare. That left just enough time to make two fat toasted sandwiches with whatever goodies we found in the fridge.

We'd take the tray up to my room and kick off our shoes. Then we'd throw ourselves down on my old cushions, hit the button on the TV remote and let the theme tune surge into the room. And we'd both sigh with pure happiness.

First came the piano, then the saxophone. But it was really the violins that swept us up and away, like surfers catching a huge wave.

This wasn't any TV soap. It was our magic carpet, floating me and Karen out of dead-end Greybridge and into the wonderful world of *Paradise High*. We never *meant* to sing along with the theme like morons, but we always did. '*Every day is paradise in Paradise Bay,*' we crooned. It's true.

Paradise Bay is the loveliest place on earth. For one thing, it's always summer, so everything looks golden; as if it's been drenched in honey. And all the people have such exciting lives. Most kids who go to Paradise High School don't even live with their real parents.

Havana (my best character) lives by herself. She moved into this lonely windmill after she found out her mum wasn't her real mother, after all. No one minds her living alone. I think everyone can see she's dead unusual because she stays awake all night writing romantic songs about nature.

'Why couldn't you call me something beautiful like Havana?' I used to moan at my parents. 'Instead of a stupid name like Lizzy Lemon.'

Some nights Havana actually sings at a really cool cafe called the Pit Stop. That cafe is open twenty-four hours a day, just about.

The kids from *Paradise High* buy breakfast there on their way to school. Then after lessons, they crowd in to order massive knickerbocker glories. No one eats them though. After the first mouthful, someone always rushes out crying, because of finding a long-lost twin their parents forgot to mention.

Mum couldn't understand what I saw in it.

'Soaps rot your brains. They're nothing like real life,' she nagged. Not like my life, she meant.

Dead right. I'd lived in the same house with the same parents in the same boring street in Greybridge since I was born. And the most exciting thing that ever happened was when our chip pan caught fire.

Sometimes, when I thought about how boring I was, compared to Havana, this horrible, empty feeling washed over me. The way it did when the credits began to roll and we had another long week to wait for the next episode of *Paradise High*.

That's one reason why I started to video it. Also, it's surprising how many little things you miss the first time.

At school, Karen always sat next to me so we could carry on dreaming about *Paradise High*. It's a bit embarrassing to explain, but sometimes we pretended we were in it. You know, actual characters. Karen's favourite girl in *Paradise High* was Scarlet.

Personally, I thought Scarlet was dead selfish, but Karen said she was a caring person, deep down.

It was weird, if I thought about it. Because my character and Karen's were best friends, like me and Karen. And sometimes when we talked about them, Scarlet and Havana seemed so close I could almost reach out and touch them. As if they were my real actual friends!

Karen was the only other person who knew what *Paradise High* meant to me. That's why we hung around together. Most of the time I thought Karen was a real laugh. And if she went into one of her little sulks, I'd just mention Calvin and she cheered up in no time.

Calvin is that tough boy in *Paradise High*; the one whose father escaped from prison, and made Calvin hot-wire a stolen car. Calvin's a genius with car engines but he gets dead moody at school. Then Scarlet found out it was because he never learned to read properly.

Karen wanted Calvin and Scarlet to get together. But in one episode, Calvin got a bit confused about his criminal past, so he kissed Ruby at the school dance, right in front of everyone!

'But Scarlet taught him to write his name,' Karen wailed. 'She bought a new dress specially for that dance. He was meant to kiss *her*, not that prune-faced Ruby.'

I've tried explaining to Karen about plots.

How it's never so exciting if the story works out the way you think it's going to. But she couldn't get the hang of it. So to distract her I said cunningly, 'If Calvin met you, he'd like you best anyway.'

Karen went quiet. Then she said, 'I do look like Scarlet now I'm growing my hair, don't I?'

I hoped Karen would say I look like Havana too, but she went back to fretting about Calvin.

Miss Finch used to say Karen had pink marshmallow between her ears instead of brains. I don't think she liked Karen much.

Miss Finch hadn't been teaching at our school long, so she still tried to get us interested in lessons. I think I might have actually enjoyed English, if everyone would've shut up. But Karen said Miss Finch was really sad for wearing the wrong colours for her skin type, and reading poetry.

Everyone else agreed about the poetry. But I'd noticed that Havana's songs sounded quite poetic before she put them to music.

If I read poetry, maybe I'd be able to write songs as good as Havana's? I didn't mention this to Karen though. Wanting to write songs was my deadly secret.

Poor Miss Finch had this little mousy voice. Every time she spoke, the boys made zoo noises – and worse – to drown her out. You couldn't hear a word; only see her mouth moving. She was like this shy little fish in a tank full of killer piranhas. I couldn't bear to watch.

The girls never joined in though. We used to swap magazines and read till the bell went. Then one day Miss Finch said, 'May I see, Lizzy?' And she whisked my brand new *Mizz* out of my hands. It was a special *Paradise High* issue.

I was scared she was going to rip it up in front of me and say I had marshmallow between my ears too. Instead, she flicked through the pages as if she was looking for something. Sure enough, when she reached the pictures of Havana, Miss Finch smiled.

'She's a character in *Paradise High*, isn't she?' she said. 'Do any of you watch that soap?'

'Duh,' said Karen. 'It's only the best thing on the telly.'

Then Miss Finch said something unbelievable. 'I know one of the writers, actually,' she said in her soft little voice. 'Harvey Spangler. He's coming over to England from Australia for a few days. Would you like him to come and talk to you?'

Everyone went wild. Even the boys. We pestered Miss Finch for the rest of the lesson. We wanted to know *everything* about Harvey Spangler.

'You won't believe this, but he's just ordinary,' Miss Finch said.

'He grew up in a town like Greybridge. You could be every bit as successful as he is, if you really want to.'

'Right, Miss,' grinned Karen. Everyone knew no one interesting came from dead-end Greybridge.

Karen and I badgered Miss Finch every day to make sure she didn't forget. When she came in on Monday morning, she was all smiles.

'Harvey's popping in after lunch,' she said. 'He can only spare us an hour as he's flying back to Sydney tonight. I know I don't have to ask you to be on your best behaviour while he's with this class.'

Karen glowered at Ash Palmer. 'So no ape noises.'

Karen and I were too excited to eat.

When the bell went we hurtled into class and bagged seats at the front.

'We're his *real* fans,' whispered Karen. 'The others are only copying.'

The door opened and an incredibly tall man followed Miss Finch into the room.

He had floppy hair like a film star and he was wearing faded jeans and a nice jacket over his white T-shirt.

He looked completely wonderful, not scruffy at all. And when he smiled, his eyes were this dazzling blue, like the ocean at Paradise Bay.

Harvey Spangler was in our actual classroom! It was like a dream.

Only, suddenly, my heart was beating too fast. My hands were sweating. I couldn't breathe. I'm *not* going to be sick, I told myself fiercely. I'd rather die. And I tried to swallow. Then I tried to stand up. But the room went all funny.

So instead I did the stupidest thing I've ever done in my life. I crumpled off my chair like a rag doll. I'd fainted.

2

Star dust

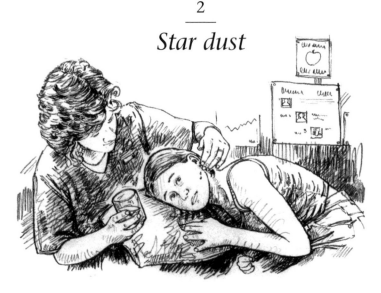

I came round to find Miss Simpson, our school secretary, splashing my face with cold water.

At first I couldn't understand what I was doing in the medical room; then I burst out crying. I'd missed the best moment of my life. To make it worse, Karen didn't even come and see how I was.

Miss Finch popped in between lessons and my heart gave a mad leap, until I saw she was on her own.

'I'm afraid Harvey had to rush off in a taxi,' she said. 'But he specially asked me to give you this.'

I sat up and clutched my head. I was still really woozy. Miss Finch held out a piece of blue paper with loopy gold scribbles all over it. I took it without thinking. Then I saw what it said.

To Lizzy Lemon with love
from Harvey Spangler.

'There wasn't time for everyone to get autographs,' Miss Finch explained. 'But Harvey wanted you to have something to remember him by.'

I stared at it. My name looked quite different in Harvey's round gold writing. Not stupid at all. Actually, it looked as if it belonged to someone rather special. A gentle glow started somewhere inside my chest.

'Poor Lizzy,' said Miss Finch. 'You must feel miserable.'

I was still staring at my name. 'Oh, that's all right,' I said. 'I don't mind.' It was true.

Harvey Spangler had given me my own little piece of *Paradise High*. It was almost worth fainting for.

Miss Finch said I'd better stay where I was till home time. 'We don't want you walking under lorries.' So I dozed a bit. Then I woke up and had delicious drifty daydreams about Paradise Bay. Five seconds after the bell went, Karen burst in. 'Feeling better?' she asked.

'Yes. Look.' I showed her my autograph.

'Oh, that. Wait till you see what I've got,' gloated Karen. She hunted in her bag.

Karen has to go one better. She can't stand anyone else to be the special one. She has to be the centre of attention all the time. 'That autograph was my idea, anyway,' she said. 'And you'll never guess what he left behind!' She opened her hand. 'Ta da!'

It was the most beautiful pen I'd ever seen: a delicate silvery-green like that smooth glass you get washed up on the beach.

'It's got a window in the barrel,' Karen said. 'Look.'

She shook it and glittering, gold grains went soaring about inside the window. Somehow they made me think of golden angels in a tiny, trapped heaven.

Karen's eyes were shining. 'Wait till you hear the best part. This is only his lucky pen that he writes all the *Paradise High* episodes with. And we've got it, Lizzy! You and me!'

'He'll be on the plane now,' I said. 'Miss will have to send it to him in Australia.'

'You don't think we're going to tell *her?*' said Karen. 'People like him can buy lucky pens any time they want. The way I see it, he's had his turn. We're the ones that need the luck.'

Karen made it sound like borrowing someone's video card. I wasn't sure we could help ourselves to someone's luck like that.

'Because it's lucky for him, it doesn't mean it'll work for us,' I pointed out. 'Maybe he only *thinks* it's lucky.'

Karen shook her head. 'Ever since he's had this pen, he says, everything he does is a thumping success. He's made so much money, he could retire. But he's having too much fun. Can't you see, Lizzy! We deserve this pen.'

'Do we?' I thought Karen sounded frighteningly like Scarlet does when she wants something that doesn't belong to her.

'Of course we do. We've watched every episode of his soap since it started. We're his biggest fans. If Harvey Spangler knew, I bet he'd *give* us his flipping pen himself. I wouldn't be surprised if he left it behind on purpose.' Karen even looked like Scarlet now: sort of sly and foxy.

'What's the point?' I said. 'You can't bring it to school. Miss Finch would recognize it. What will you do with it?'

'What will *we* do,' Karen corrected me. 'It's ours, Lizzy. For you and me to share for ever. I've got it all worked out. And when I tell you my idea, you're going to die!' She dropped her voice.

'We're going to buy a notebook and we'll write our *own* soap! And they'll put it on TV and we'll be rich and famous like Harvey.'

I couldn't believe what I was hearing. 'What – write it with his pen?'

'Duh!' said Karen, grinning at me. 'No, with my little finger. What do you think I meant, Lizzy Lemon!'

Just listening to Karen scared me silly. At the same time, I badly wanted to believe her. If we were rich and famous like Harvey Spangler, we could get out of Greybridge. We could live somewhere wonderful like Paradise Bay. Not for a measly half hour once a week, but for ever.

So I did what Havana does when she lets Scarlet talk her into something dangerous. I bit my lip and nodded dead slowly. Karen burst out laughing. She hugged me so hard I felt my ribs crunch. We both screamed with excitement.

'Honestly, that's so brilliant, Karen,' I told her. Then I remembered.

'I've got the perfect notebook already! It was in my Christmas stocking. It's even gold. Karen, that's so spooky. Like it was *meant.*'

When we got back to my house, we didn't make sandwiches. We didn't even watch last week's *Paradise High* on video. We went straight up to my room. 'Okay,' Karen said when we'd found my notebook, 'start writing, babe.' Scarlet calls Havana 'babe'. Karen thought it sounded dead cool.

'We can't just start. We have to plan it first. What it's called; where it's set. First we've got to think up some characters.'

'Why?' asked Karen. 'We know them already. Scarlet, Havana and Calvin and all the other kids at Paradise High.'

I stared at her. 'But that's not our soap.'

'We'll make it ours. We'll write new adventures for them – more exciting ones. We can't go wrong with this pen. Trust me.'

A shiver ran down my back. 'Trust me' is what people in soaps say just before everything goes incredibly wrong.

But Karen seemed so sure of herself, I wanted to believe her. 'We do know an awful lot about Paradise Bay,' I said, cautiously.

'We know everything, babe,' said Karen in her scary Scarlet voice. 'And now that Scarlet and Havana are going to get the best stories, *Paradise High* will be a better soap than ever.'

I could see a teeny problem here. You see, what I hadn't told Karen was that I'd always fancied Calvin too. No matter who wrote the stories, Scarlet and Havana couldn't *both* get him. And I knew Havana wouldn't get a look in if Karen had anything to do with it.

'Let me think about it,' I said. 'Let's make those sandwiches after all. I promise I'll come up with some good ideas by tomorrow.' I'd never been firm with Karen before. She usually bossed *me*.

'All right,' she moaned, 'so long as Scarlet gets some really juicy scenes! You'd better keep the pen though. I don't want one of my brothers to nick it. But don't write anything without me, okay!'

I couldn't sleep that night. Even after Mum and Dad came upstairs, I tossed and turned. Finally I slid the pen from under my pillow. 'Is it you keeping me awake?' I whispered.

I gasped as the street light caught it, filling it with glittering star-dust. And then I knew why I couldn't sleep and why I kept thinking about beautiful, impossible things like angels and star-dust. Every speck of gold inside Harvey Spangler's pen was an untold story, waiting to be written down.

I couldn't help it. I knew I'd promised to wait, but I had to try it out.

I switched on my lamp, reached for my golden notebook and began to write the words exactly as Harvey's pen put them into my head.

'Havana had been up all night working on a new love song, even though she could never sing it to the boy of her dreams. For the first time in her life she overslept. By the time she'd put on one of her long, romantic, second-hand dresses, she was so late she had to run for the bus.

Then she dropped her bag and everything fell out. But someone said, "Let me help you." Looking up, Havana found herself gazing into the laughing eyes of the most amazing boy she'd ever seen …'

I never knew writing stories was so easy. The right words spilled into my mind like golden beads. All I had to do was keep threading them, one after another. By the time the pen slid out of my hand, I'd filled three whole pages with tiny, gold writing.

And while I slept, everything around me began to change.

3

The amazing imaginary boy

A bird was screeching in our lilac tree. I
opened my eyes and saw a flash of emerald
wings. Mrs Harris's parrot was out again.

My room was incredibly sunny. I had to
squint against the light to read the numbers
on my clock radio. Then I saw the time. I'd
overslept!

I threw on the first clothes I could find,
stuffed the pen in my bag, and dashed
downstairs.

I'd have to find a new notebook for our soap. Even though my story was about Havana, not me, I couldn't bring myself to show it to Karen, somehow.

There was no sign of my parents anywhere. Mum and Dad never normally go out early without telling me. They hadn't even left a note; I felt quite hurt actually. But I plastered some bread with a dark, grungy spread I found in the fridge, and dashed out of the house. The bread was so disgusting, I dropped it in a bin on the way. What's Mum thinking of, I wondered. Isn't Vegemite the stuff Australians are all crazy about?

You'll think I'm incredibly dim, but I really didn't guess what had happened. I noticed it was hot though, because I was glad I'd worn that strange floaty dress I found on my chair. And I did jump when a sun-tanned boy whizzed past on a skateboard, shouting, 'Loved your singing last week.' But I just thought it was one of Karen's brothers having a laugh.

Then suddenly, I stopped dead.

Incredibly, someone had squeezed a whole new building between the post office and the launderette!

Yesterday I'd have sworn there wasn't enough room for a phone box. It wasn't the usual Greybridge horror either. This building was wooden and painted in zippy bright sea and sunflower colours. The door stood slightly open. I could smell coffee and delicious vanilla smells. It was a new cafe!

I couldn't believe a place this cool was opening in our town! Wait till I told Karen. Then I saw what it was called: THE PIT STOP. *No*, I thought. What a coincidence! You'd think I'd have caught on then, but I didn't.

A girl in cutoffs and a tiny t-shirt came out and propped up a blackboard. *TODAY'S SPECIALS*, it said. I was hopelessly late but I just had to read what the specials were – *Double Crust Blueberry Pie*. I'd never eaten blueberries, but I knew they'd taste wonderful.

The girl went back inside, leaving the door wide open.

I could see right into the sunlit cafe with its leafy ferns and whirling ceiling fans. For some reason the girl and her *Specials* board and the dazzling sea-blue chairs and tables seemed strangely familiar. But everything seemed strange today, as if I was drifting through a summery gold dream.

Suddenly, I noticed a bus waiting at the stop. It dawned on me that if I caught it, I wouldn't be late for school after all. I tore after it and just managed to jump on before it sailed away.

Unfortunately, I dropped my bag. Everything flew out over the floor. But a voice said, 'Let me help you.' And looking up, I found myself staring into the laughing eyes of the most amazing boy I'd ever seen.

I'd never met him before. But I knew his face as well as my own. It was the boy I'd made up. The boy from my story.

I snatched my things back and fled to the back of the bus. My face was burning. My golden dream had just turned into the darkest of nightmares. I should never have let Karen talk me into it, I told myself. I'd figured out by then that the stolen pen was to blame, of course. How else could some boy I'd invented last night, appear on a real life Greybridge bus and do and say exactly what he'd said and done in my story?

My heart was thumping like crazy. I glanced round. The amazing boy was chatting to kids from my school, just like a real person. Maybe if I ignored him, he'd vanish as mysteriously as he came. I stared out of the bus and began counting slowly to a hundred.

When I reached 'nine', I was puzzled to see Mrs Harris's parrot again, perching on some telephone wires. Then there was a flurry of wings and five emerald-green birds blinked back at me. Five escaped parrots? Even *I* didn't believe that. They're not tame at all, I thought, in a blur of terror. They're wild!

Now when wild parrots start flying around Greybridge, even I know something's up. Next minute, the driver braked hard. Everyone went sliding all over the bus. 'Flaming menace,' he growled, 'someone ought to tell the council.'

The passengers picked themselves up. No one else even glanced at the large animal bouncing calmly down Greybridge High Street. But I was shaking all over.

When I got off, I was in such a state I didn't see the tough-looking boy zoom past on roller-blades. Someone yanked me out of the way. 'Hey, Calvin!' he yelled. 'Look where you're going, mate.' The imaginary boy had rescued me again! For some reason I acted just as bashful as if he was a real person. I turned bright red, mumbled something stupid, and ran into school.

I was faintly surprised to see all the girls were wearing gingham dresses and straw hats today. Only really sad kids wear the uniform at our school usually, and anyway, surprise

surprise, it's grey. But then I saw my own reflection in the trophy cupboard and went into total shock.

I reached up to touch my hair. It was chin-length yesterday. It's been that length since I *had* hair. Now it tumbled over my shoulders in romantic waves, like Havana's.

I gazed down at my strange, floaty dress. For the first time, I saw it was identical to the one Havana wore in the last episode.

Honestly, I nearly fainted all over again, but a familiar voice chirped, 'Hiya, babe.'

'Karen!' I almost wept with relief. 'You're the same at least.'

But she wasn't. Not really. For one thing, she was wearing a gingham dress. And she'd put these little plaits in her hair, like Scarlet's.

I told myself this was just coincidence. Karen was my best friend, wasn't she? At least the two of us were in this together.

'This is my fault, Karen,' I burbled. 'I used our pen and – well, its powers are more incredible than we thought.' I gave a nervous giggle. 'Can you believe someone's opened a cafe called the Pit Stop? And our bus driver nearly ran over a kangaroo. Plus, I actually saw Calvin.'

Karen didn't seem to hear. 'You left your hat behind last night, babe,' she said. She handed me a hat with daisies on it.

I've only seen two people wear hats like that: Eliza Dolittle in *My Fair Lady*, and Havana in *Paradise High*.

'Karen, we need to talk,' I said urgently. I dragged her into the girls' toilets. 'This has gone too far. We've got to stop it right now. I know Greybridge looks wonderful – sunshine and parrots and everything. But none of it's *real*, can't you see? I'm scared. I want my old life back.' My eyes were full of tears.

Karen checked her reflection in the mirror, smiling Scarlet's foxy little smile.

I felt a surge of panic. 'You *are* still Karen, aren't you?'

She tossed her plaits. 'Last time I looked.'

'And we're best friends?'

'Of course, babe. Friends for ever.'

'So who am I? What's my name?'

'You stayed up late writing romantic songs again, Lizzy, didn't you?' said Karen soothingly.

'You called me Lizzy! So I'm still Lizzy Lemon, right?' I was so grateful, I felt my knees go to jelly.

'You're acting really strange, Lizzy, you know?' Karen twiddled one plait, moodily. 'Listen, babe,' she said, 'I'll buy you some of Angie's blueberry pie at the Pit Stop after school. Till then, try to be a bit less *intense*, can't you. People will start to think you're weird.' And frowning her new cute little frown, Karen flounced through the door.

I followed her but my head was spinning.

What was going on? If I was still Lizzy and Karen was Karen, why did we look like Scarlet and Havana? Why had Greybridge been transformed into a tropical paradise? Strangest of all, why didn't anyone notice these terrifying changes except me? Unless …

On either side of the corridor, kids crashed their locker doors happily. They didn't seem to know we never even had lockers at our school until today. At Greybridge High you have to drag your stuff round with you all day like a donkey. It's Paradise High that has lockers.

I heard Karen whisper, 'Someone should contact Lizzy's dad.'

'I think he's still on safari with his new supermodel girlfriend,' Amanda hissed back.

But by then I'd worked it out.

It was terrifying being the only person in Greybridge who knew the truth. Everyone else was so busy being a character in *Paradise High*, it didn't occur to them it wasn't real.

But I knew better. I'd trapped an entire town inside an Australian soap opera by mistake. The trouble was, I hadn't the faintest idea what to do about it.

4

Harvey Spangler's soap spell

Most mornings at Greybridge High, our teachers huddle in the staff room over their cups of coffee, till the bell goes and they have to come out and teach us. You can hear them moaning about their pay and how they're getting flu. Greybridge teachers almost always have flu.

So when I glanced in on the way to class, I nearly had heart failure.

Harvey Spangler's pen had sprinkled its star-dust over my teachers too. You'd think the women had just stepped out of the beauty parlour. And the men looked like hunky ski instructors, even Mr Horne! But it wasn't just that. It wasn't even their new glamorous clothes. It was the teachers themselves. They *glowed*. Overnight, they'd suddenly turned into gorgeous superstars!

And it wasn't just how they looked either. When they opened their mouths, these dead wise sayings came out. 'Teaching is the most important job in the world,' sang Mrs Henny. Then she went on about our young minds unfolding. Was this the same Mrs Henny who told Ash Palmer he had less sense than a chimps' tea party?

One teacher wore a stunning silk outfit that showed miles of leg. She was arguing with Mr Griffin, our head.

I'd rather pick a fight with Darth Vader, personally, but she was outrageous. 'I respect your views, Paul,' she said in a firm voice.

'But this will be *A Midsummer Night's Dream* as it's never been done before. A musical, using their own music.' She waved her manicured hands. 'Rap, drum and bass and …'

And suddenly I knew who she was! 'Blimey, it's Miss Finch,' I breathed. 'But I could hear every word!'

Karen's eyes were soft with longing. 'Oh, Lizzy,' she said. 'I hope Miss Finch picks me for her play. She's so-o inspiring.'

I decided to try an experiment. 'Karen,' I said. 'Have you heard of someone called Harvey Spangler?'

She crinkled her forehead. 'Isn't he that famous dress designer?'

'He writes soaps,' I said. 'You borrowed his lucky pen?'

She couldn't take it in though. Like everyone else in Greybridge, Karen was under Harvey Spangler's soap spell. But spells can be broken, I thought. The trouble was, it looked as if I was the only one in a fit state to do it. Then suddenly, I knew what I had to do.

The minute school was over, I'd run down to the post office and post that trouble-making pen back to Australia out of harm's way.

And tomorrow Greybridge will be back to normal, I thought. I've just got to get through today. For once I was looking forward to double maths. It was just what I needed, something deadly dull to calm me down.

That's what I thought anyway, until the teacher marched in and wrote the first problem on the board. Honestly, I nearly died. Maybe a Martian kid from the next century could understand that kind of stuff, but it didn't mean a thing to me. But everyone else just chewed their pens and looked dead intelligent, as if they did Martian algebra every day.

I was still in shock when nice, dull, quiet Mr Rawlins started ranting about how he'd always wanted to be an artist when he was a kid, but his dad said he didn't have a talented bone in his body.

'Well, I'm going to prove my father wrong,' he shouted. And he threw down his chalk, wrapped this kind of swooshy silk scarf around his neck, and stormed out.

'He's completely flipped,' I whispered to Karen.

Karen ruled a neat line across a totally empty page. 'I think it's wonderful,' she said. 'He's gone home to do art, and be kind to his own kids before it's too late.'

Just then, out of the corner of my eye, I saw something swoop across the playground. It was Calvin on his roller-blades. As I watched, he turned and angrily shook his fist. Then he zoomed through the school gate like a streak of lightning. Karen gasped and stared helplessly after him.

Then Jody said, 'I hear Calvin was in the Pit Stop last night trying to sell a stereo. And wouldn't we like to know where he got that?'

'He didn't steal it, if that's what you mean,' Karen cried. 'Calvin's changed, I know he has.'

It was amazing. No one said, 'Isn't Calvin just some bloke in a soap?' or, 'Calvin can't possibly have been in the Pit Stop yesterday, dummy, because yesterday it didn't actually exist.' They totally believed what they were saying.

Then the bell went and Miss Finch swept in. 'Sorry everyone, no poetry today,' she cried. 'Just kidding. I've got an exciting project I want to discuss with you all.'

Everyone listened admiringly as she described her trendy musical. But I just chewed my nails, dying for the lesson to be over. Miss Finch was my only hope of getting Harvey Spangler's address. As everyone crowded out of the room, I went up to her. 'I need a favour, Miss.'

She smiled. 'I wanted to catch you too, Lizzy,' she said. 'You're such a talented singer, I'd like your help with our production.'

'Okay,' I heard myself say casually. 'I'll write the songs too, if you like.'

Can you *believe* I said that! It's not as if I'm lying, I told myself. Lies only count in real life. And if I do her a favour, the chances are, she'll do me one back.

'Oh, Miss, I wanted your friend's address,' I said in my confident Havana voice, 'so I can thank him for his interesting talk.'

'Friend?' she echoed. Poor Miss Finch looked like a sleepwalker who isn't quite ready to wake up. I couldn't blame her. She was having loads more fun in this soap than she did in real life.

'Your friend Harvey Spangler? Maybe it's in your filofax,' I hinted.

Her face cleared. 'Of course, Lizzy.' She scrabbled in her bag. 'Here's one of his cards. Send him my love, won't you?'

'Thanks, Miss,' I said, gleefully.

As I was leaving, Miss Finch said, 'Lizzy, are you really all right, living in that lonely old windmill?' She meant it too. Just like the real shy Miss Finch would.

'Couldn't be better, Miss,' I said. I popped Harvey Spangler's card in the pocket of Havana's dress. 'Thanks, Miss.'

'Oh, Lizzy,' Miss Finch called after me. 'You forgot your hat.'

I went back for it, laughing. Now I wasn't trapped in a soap for ever, I felt brilliant. I danced down the corridor, humming. For a whole sixty seconds I felt just like the talented unusual girl everyone thought I was.

You'd think I'd remember, wouldn't you? Every single time someone's in a great mood in a soap, something incredibly dark happens in the very next scene. Suddenly, Karen ran up to me, tears streaming down her face.

'Lizzy – Calvin's been expelled!'

'Why?' I said, trying to sound amazed. It was amazing, actually. Calvin doesn't go to our school.

'He refused to take his earring out when Mr Griffin told him to,' she wept. 'And that's not all. That rich kid at Whitegrove High, Neville? The one they call Twister? Well he challenged Calvin to a roller-blade competition after school and Calvin agreed. He's so upset, he might do something crazy.'

'But Calvin's a brilliant roller-blader,' I said.

'The best in Paradi – in Greybridge.'

'Lizzy, Neville's a roller-blade genius but he's also as twisted as his name. He'll do anything it takes to beat Calvin. Everyone knows Calvin's only got battered old roller-blades. He could get hurt trying to copy those dangerous stunts Neville does. Lizzy, we've got to stop him before it's too late. You've got to come with me, now.'

'You mean bunk off school!' I said, horrified. Then I remembered none of this was happening. Bunking off didn't count. Karen and I could have a wonderful adventure in Paradise Bay like we always dreamed!

I haven't forgotten my promise, honestly, I told myself. The minute we've finished helping Calvin I really will send that pen back.

I knew I had to help Karen though. Havana always helps Scarlet, no matter how much trouble they get in later.

We stole out of school and into the sunny streets. I can't tell you how wicked it felt – wicked, and ever so exciting.

Greybridge looked really pretty. There was this soft, gold shimmer everywhere. I knew perfectly well that Harvey Spangler's soap spell was causing it, but it was still lovely. As we passed the Pit Stop, Angie waved.

'Have you seen Calvin?' Karen yelled.

Angie came out. 'Shouldn't you two be in school?' Then she grinned. 'That boy's in trouble again, is he? Have you tried the beach?'

'The beach?' I repeated, blankly. In real life Greybridge is as far from the sea as you can get.

'Cut through the cafe if you like.' And Angie pointed through the open patio doors at the back of the Pit Stop.

I stared in amazement at the white beach with its great, blue waves sweeping in and out. It looked so exactly like the opening titles to *Paradise High*, I almost cried. After today all this would vanish for ever. And so would Karen's one chance of making Calvin fall in love with her.

To my alarm, I suddenly found myself making a bargain. All right, Lizzy Lemon, I said. This is how it's going to be. We'll save Calvin from the evil roller-blade genius, have a paddle in that lovely blue sea, try a slice of Angie's pie, and *then* I'll post the pen back – cross my heart and hope to die.

And before I lost my nerve, I pulled Karen into Angie's cafe and straight out the other side.

Warm salt-wind whipped our hair: a gull cried overhead. A boy stood on the seashore, flicking stones across the water. We ran towards him, breathlessly. He turned and smiled at me, a truly dazzling smile. My heart skipped a beat.

'Who's *that*?' scowled Karen.

And it wasn't Calvin at all. It was my imaginary boy.

5

Never order a knickerbocker glory

Whenever anything embarrassing happens in
Paradise High, the characters freeze like
statues, and stare moodily at each other until
the adverts come on.

And funnily enough, that's exactly what
happened when Karen and I bumped into the
mysterious boy; only without any helpful
commercials.

I knew I should introduce them, but what
could I say? 'Karen, this is that boy I invented
for Havana without telling you!'

She wouldn't take it in now, because of the soap spell, but as soon as Greybridge was back to normal she'd figure it out: I knew she would.

I never meant to fill our town with kangaroos, or for me and Karen to swap lives with two soap characters. But that wouldn't make any difference to Karen. She'd think I was trying to get one up on her. It's not nice to say, but Karen's not a very forgiving girl. If she ever realized what I'd done, I'd have to find a new best friend.

The three of us would probably still be standing there like waxworks, but suddenly a huge wave came streaking up the sand. We jumped out of the way and after that everybody kind of unfroze.

'You must be Karen,' said the boy. 'Lizzy talks about you heaps. So does Calvin,' he added, smiling. Karen didn't smile back.

'Angie told us Calvin was on the beach,' I stammered. I was having a bit of trouble holding Havana's flowery hat on in the breeze.

'I saw him heading for the dolphin pool,'
he said.

'I never heard Lizzy mention you,' Karen
said, frowning. The new Karen didn't seem
much different to the old Karen in that way.
They both hated me to have any life of my
own.

'Oh, we go way back,' he said, airily. 'Still
on for singing at Angie's surprise party this
evening, Lizzy?'

'Er – I'm not sure actually,' I said, trying to
sound as if people ask me to sing at surprise
parties every day. But my mind went into red
alert. Forget the roller-blade war, it screamed,
forget the pie. Post that pen pronto, before
it's too late.

The boy laughed. I got the feeling he was enjoying this. 'If it makes you feel better, let's go and rehearse.'

'But we've got to find Calvin,' I stuttered. *And I know I look like Havana today. But I'm just Lizzy. Boring Lizzy Lemon.*

'I'll help you find him,' he said. 'Then we'll rehearse, okay?'

'Okay,' I squeaked. So the three of us crunched along the shore. Soon we saw a sun-bleached signpost saying, *TO THE DOLPHINS*. Karen went storming ahead like someone in *Mission Impossible*.

'I'm Jake Cutter, by the way,' the boy murmured. I thought it was lovely of him to wait till Karen couldn't hear. Then my jaw dropped. Jake has to be my favourite boy's name of all time. The spooky thing is, in my story, I never actually got round to giving Havana's new love interest a name at all! But that's nothing to what happened next.

'Here, take this,' he said. 'It fell out of your bag this morning. I thought you'd need it.'

And Jake gave me back Harvey Spangler's pen. Honestly, my hair nearly stood on end. I'd lost the darn thing and never noticed! Suppose I'd never run into him again? What then?

Then it dawned on me: Jake knew I'd turn up on the beach. The way he knew about our craze for *Paradise High*, and the stolen pen, and my secret wish to be like Havana. If you ask me, Jake Cutter knew me better than *I* did.

I was so ashamed. It was worse than that dream about going to school in my underwear. But Jake didn't seem bothered at all. So after I got over the shock, I stopped bothering too. We took off our shoes and splashed along by the edge of the sea. The water was so clear, you could see rainbows in it. Then Jake said, 'So you're sending it back tonight?'

'I'd have sent it before,' I said, 'but I promised we'd help Calvin.'

'Figured out how this mix-up happened yet?' he said, casually.

I shrugged, 'Nope,' then I giggled. 'Actually I feel a bit like Mickey Mouse, trying to stop the sorcerer's brooms wrecking everything.'

Jake examined a stranded starfish. 'Magic is like music,' he said, 'you have to practise to get it right.' He gently flipped the tiny creature into a rock pool. 'So why not practise till it's time to send the pen back.'

I stared. 'You mean, use it to help Calvin beat Evil Neville for Karen? What a cool idea! Can the pen do that?'

He sighed. 'You don't get it, do you?' he said. 'Lizzy, this story we're in together – it isn't Harvey Spangler's story or the magic pen's, you know. It's *yours*. Okay?'

'Mine?' I said, alarmed at the idea I had anything to do with it. I giggled nervously. 'You're just kidding, right? *Right?*'

I followed him anxiously up sandy, wooden steps. At the top, we found Karen dangling her bare feet into an open-air pool, and gazing at Calvin, misty-eyed. Personally, I couldn't remember what I'd seen in him.

But he did look dead sweet playing with those dolphins. Not tough and moody at all.

I should have guessed Calvin would be here, really. He rushes off to be with the dolphins every time he's upset in *Paradise High*. Deep down, you see, Calvin wants to do marine biology, only he's scared he's not smart enough.

'Have you talked to him?' I whispered. Karen shook her head.

'I've got a brilliant plan, but I can't talk about it, okay? Tell Calvin we'll treat him at Angie's, after his swim.'

She frowned. 'If your idea is so brilliant, why can't you tell me?'

'Trust me,' I grinned. I wasn't lying. It was brilliant. But I couldn't exactly tell Karen I was going to win Calvin's roller-blade battle for him, could I? Well, I was doing it for her really. I felt I owed her somehow. So after Calvin finished his swim, we walked back up the beach to the Pit Stop.

'Four shakes, Angie, and four slices of blueberry pie,' said Jake.

The old Karen would have been thrilled to sit at one of those sea-blue tables like an actual character in *Paradise High*. But the new Karen seemed to think she did this every day. 'I don't want pie or a shake, thanks. I want a knickerbocker glory,' she snapped.

But I was sure this was absolutely the worst thing she could do. 'No, don't, Karen,' I pleaded. 'Have anything else on the menu but not that.' She must be kidding! Whenever anyone in *Paradise High* has a knickerbocker glory, all hell breaks loose!

'Why ever not?' she said in surprise.

'Because – there's so many calories in them,' I invented, wildly.

'Who are you, the diet police?' Karen jeered. 'If I want calories, babe, I'll flipping have them, okay!'

'Put your money away, kids, it's on the house,' said Angie.

'Have you got some old menus or something, Angie?' I asked. 'I want to write something down before I forget it.'

'Lizzy's got one of her songs coming on again,' said Karen, making song-writing sound like a virus. I didn't tell her it wasn't songs I had in mind.

Angie handed me a stack of menus. 'Be my guest, chick.'

Our food arrived. Angie's blueberry pie turned out to be pure heaven on a plate. I'd have enjoyed it even more if I hadn't been so nervous about Karen and her knickerbocker glory. She messed around with it for ages, picking off the cherries one by one.

Was she going to eat the thing or not?

Then to my alarm, Karen suddenly dug her spoon right in, closed her eyes and slurped up a huge, delicious mouthful.

Jake pulled a face. 'She can't say you didn't warn her,' he whispered.

A girl in a tight red dress sauntered in and walked up to the counter. 'Sure,' I heard Angie say, 'she's over there.' The girl swung round. The resemblance really was incredible. Even Calvin choked on his pie, and he ought to be used to it by now. 'This is unreal,' he spluttered. 'Karen, she's your double!'

Karen gasped. 'It can't be true!'

The girl smiled spitefully. 'It can and it is,' she said. 'I'm Kelly, your long lost twin sister. I've come for my share of our inheritance.'

Karen's lip quivered. 'I'm going to find Mum!' She ran out of the cafe, sobbing.

'Karen, wait!' cried Calvin, and then he rushed off after *her*.

'Who's that?' Kelly asked, staring admiringly after Calvin. I just glared. 'Forget it, I'll find out,' she said. And Karen's wicked twin sauntered away to cause more trouble.

Angie took away their dishes. 'Maybe I should stop serving those things,' she sighed.

I jumped up from the table. 'I'd better go after them.'

Jake pulled me down again. 'If you really want to help Karen, then stay right where you are, pick up that pen and write the next episode of your story.'

'But it's getting so complicated. I don't even know what I want to happen!' I wailed.

'Then get writing, Lizzy Lemon, and find out.' He sounded so confident, I almost believed what he was saying. So right there in Angie's famous cafe, I clicked open Harvey Spangler's pen, and started writing.

6

The blade zone

It wasn't like the first time; when all the right words slid smoothly into my mind like golden beads, and I simply strung them together. For one thing the Pit Stop was the very worst place to concentrate.

Every few minutes, new people burst in to cry on Angie's shoulder: Mrs Rawlins for one. 'Why would someone give up a perfectly good teaching job?' she sobbed. 'He's talking about us moving to Tahiti!'

'I wish you would,' I muttered. I crumpled up my latest effort in despair.

It was different when I believed the pen was magically putting words into my head. But the truth was, the pen had only helped me write a story I already had inside me. I'd kidded myself it was about Havana and Scarlet, but deep down I always knew it was me and Karen in our soap disguises. That's why I daren't tell her about inventing Jake.

It's funny, I'm not a specially deep thinker or anything – at least I never used to be. But as I sat there with Harvey Spangler's pen in my hand, strange new ideas began popping into my head. I started thinking in a new way.

I mean, all that moaning I do about dead-end Greybridge, but when I get the chance to make my dreams come true, do I grab it with both hands? Well, actually, no. I panic about how to get my safe, boring old life back as soon as possible, that's what I do!

Then surprise, surprise, I suddenly decide it might be fun to tap into Harvey Spangler's cosmic powers after all, and why? To help Karen help a boy she fancies!

Is this because I'm a sharing person, a brilliant best friend, a saint? Not on your life. Keeping Karen happy was a habit so strong, I'd stopped noticing it. All because I'm too chicken to find out what makes me happy.

That's why I can't get started on this, I thought. Any story I write now will be mine and mine alone. And that's like admitting I want something for myself: something I don't have to share with Karen.

See what I mean! I couldn't believe the things that pen put into my head. Except they were my thoughts really. The pen just gave me courage to think them.

Jake went over to Angie's piano and began to play, soft dreamy chords. 'I'll stop if it puts you off,' he said.

'No,' I said, 'I like it.' I crossed out the sentence I'd just written and began scribbling a new one. But this time the sounds of the cafe gradually faded around me and I lost all track of time. The next time I looked up, the cafe was mellow with afternoon sunlight.

And I'd covered the backs of three menus
with gold writing.

I was worn out, but dead pleased with
myself too. I never knew writing was like
this: a long tiring journey full of surprises.
And I'd surprised myself no end!

'Finished,' I told Jake.

He came over. 'Did we all get a nice happy
ending?' he teased.

'Of course. But Jake – while I was writing I
found out all this *stuff*. I don't want a quiet
life at all! The truth is I want to be a …'

But just then a policeman came in. 'I've been hearing rumours about that young tearaway, Calvin,' he said. 'You wouldn't know anything about some stereo equipment he was trying to flog, would you?'

I collected my things together. 'Come on, Jake. I need some fresh air.'

'Drop by later, kids,' Angie called after us, as we walked out into the afternoon sunshine.

'It's my birthday today, not that you'd notice. I could do with some cheerful company.'

'Hey, Angie thinks we're cheerful company!' I said, as Jake and I headed up the High Street.

'We're the only customers who didn't either cry over her or rush out without paying.' Jake looked around him. 'Lizzy, where are we going?'

I looked at him from under my lashes, like Havana does when she's being really deep. 'You know, I've been doing all this thinking? Well, er – it made me realize there's something incredibly important I've got to do for myself before I can be any real help, you know, to other people.'

Jake nodded gravely. 'So what is it?'

I grinned. 'Buy some new clothes!' I shrieked. I grabbed him and whirled him round. 'Honestly, I feel like my own great granny in this droopy old thing. And it absolutely pongs of moth balls! I don't know how Havana stands it!'

* * *

We had a brilliant time in the shopping mall.
I even had my hair cut, well, Havana's hair.
By the time we finished, you wouldn't have
recognized us, we both looked so incredibly
cool.

But the best outfits were still in their
carrier bags. We were keeping them for later.

How did we pay for all this loot? Oh,
please! I wrote this story, remember?

There was just one thing I had to do before
we went looking for Calvin. I was quite
nervous about it, actually. But my interview
with the director of Blade City, the big roller-
blade centre, went even better than I'd
hoped. I came out with a big bag of stuff.

I glanced at my watch. 'We'd better hurry,'
I said, 'it's getting late.'

We caught up with Calvin at the seedy garage where he helps out.

'Can't stop and chat,' he scowled, 'got a little business to see to.' He wiped his oily hands and lifted some battered roller-blades down from a shelf. I didn't move. 'Private business,' he stressed, tugging off his scruffy trainers.

I dumped down a Blade City bag. 'If you're planning to win, you'd better have this. Karen said you need new blades.'

'Thanks, but I don't take charity,' said Calvin gruffly, as I knew he would. 'Why do you think I was trying to sell my own stereo last night?'

'This isn't charity,' I said. 'I didn't pay for any of this.'

Calvin frowned like a puzzled puppy. 'Then how …?'

'I told the people at Blade City they should sponsor you. The director's coming to watch. He's bringing a photographer. This is your big break, Calvin!' His mouth fell open.

'Sponsor *me*? Why would they do that?'

'Because you're the best roller-blader there is,' I said. 'So if you ask me, it's time you stopped acting like such a loser. See you around.' I took a step towards the door.

'Wait – don't go yet,' Calvin pleaded. 'Look, thanks, Lizzy. No one's ever done anything like this for me before.'

'Oh, that's okay. Anyway,' I lied, 'it was all Karen's idea. Look, we'd better go.'

'Aren't you coming to watch me?' asked Calvin. 'I'd like you to.'

'Don't worry, we won't miss your big moment, mate,' said Jake. 'Look, you get changed and we'll see you at the park, okay.'

Unless you're into scummy duck ponds, Greybridge Park isn't usually much to write home about. But today when we went through the gates, we found ourselves walking under the shade of enormous palm trees. Splashy bright flowers blazed out at us from the lush greenery. Already dozens of kids were streaming towards the blade zone.

I knew part of Paradise Park had been specially adapted for roller-blading – I'd seen it on *Paradise High*. But when you're there it's like something in a dream: with tricky ramps, curving floors that swoop up to meet the ceiling, and runways that stop dizzily in mid-air.

The place buzzed with excitement. Everyone was dying to see the battle between the strong silent kid from the wrong side of town and the twisted genius from Whitegrove. I picked Evil Neville out easily. He had white-blonde hair parted in the middle and eyes as pale as ice chips.

Then I saw the girl with him.

'That's never Karen,' I gasped. It wasn't. It was Kelly, her wicked twin. 'Well, she didn't waste much time,' I said.

'Calvin's cutting it really fine,' whispered Jake.

The Blade City man thought so too. 'What's keeping your wonder-boy, Ms Lemon?' he called across.

Neville gave his high-pitched laugh. 'Last I heard, the cops wanted the little crook for selling stolen goods.'

A shiver went down my back. 'Jake, none of this is in my story,' I whispered. 'Why is it all going so wrong?'

Five minutes ticked past. Calvin should have been here ages ago. Ten minutes. Fifteen. *Where was he?*

The man from Blade City shook his head. 'I don't like being made a fool of, Ms Lemon,' he said. And he strode away, muttering darkly into his mobile.

I watched him go, my eyes stinging. Even with cosmic powers at my disposal, I'd failed to give Karen and Calvin their happy ending. No wonder I'd been so tough on Calvin. Deep down I was a loser too.

Lizzy Lemon jumps on a hat

Suddenly Calvin was pushing his way through the crowd, closely followed by the man from Blade City.

After all the trouble I'd gone to, he'd turned up in his grungy work clothes and ancient roller-blades! His hair was plastered to his skull too, as if he'd just stuck his head under the tap.

'I got held up,' he mumbled.

I felt like hitting him. 'What happened to all your new gear, Calvin?' I said, gritting my teeth.

Calvin looked distinctly shifty. 'I, er, lost it somewhere. No sweat, I'll manage with these.' He jerked his head at Neville. 'You start while I get my breath back.'

'I hope Neville stomps him into the ground,' I whispered to Jake.

'You could give Calvin a chance to explain,' he said, as Evil Neville went storming up the walls like a daddy-long-legs on fast forward.

'Look, he's obviously sold the stuff. And he's made a complete fool of me. Just tell me one thing. If this is my story, how come Calvin messed up his own happy ending?'

Before Jake could reply, Neville dived off the top runway into a heart-stopping back flip. Seconds before he hit the ramp, he twisted sideways like a rattlesnake and landed on a different ramp, eight metres below. Then he sped away, tossing his white hair out of his eyes, having shown us how he earned his slippery nickname.

It seemed obvious Neville was going to win hands down.

'Just tell me, what did I do wrong?' I wailed.

'Nothing,' said Jake. 'You did everything exactly right.'

It was then that I noticed everyone getting restless. People started craning round, curious, as if they were expecting someone.

'… drowning,' I heard someone whisper.

'… back home for dry clothes,' muttered someone else. Suddenly, the crowd parted again, and Karen appeared. She was carrying a shivering toddler wrapped in a blanket.

'Sorry to interrupt,' she said. 'But I've got something to say to you all.'

Neville slithered to a standstill, breathing hard. 'This had better be good,' he hissed.

'I want to tell everyone why Calvin was late.'

'Karen, don't!' Calvin blurted. 'It's none of their business.'

'Yes, it is!' cried Karen, dramatically. 'I'm sick of people blaming you. I want them to know the kind of person you really are. Mum and I took my little cousin for a walk along the sea-front,' she explained. 'Mum had been keeping this big secret from me.' Karen looked daggers at Kelly here. 'So we were both a bit upset. Neither of us noticed Joey wander off. Before we could stop him, he slipped under the railings and fell into the sea. If Calvin hadn't come past …' her voice cracked, 'those sharks would have got Joey for sure.'

'Sharks!' everyone gasped.

'Oh, sure they would,' jeered Neville. 'This is so typical,' he told the watching crowd. 'The little crook knows he can't beat me, so he stages a phony rescue!'

'No, it's the truth,' said a voice. The suspicious cop from the Pit Stop shouldered his way to the front.

'This young lad dived in fully-clothed and saved the baby from drowning,' he said sternly. 'But suddenly, a bunch of man-eaters came out of nowhere. Calvin kicked off his roller-blades and used one to fight off the sharks with his free hand until help came. I wanted the doc to check him over but Calvin insisted on coming here as soon as he got a change of clothes.

'While I'm here, I'd like to say I've got a good idea who's been spreading all those lies about Calvin. Seems like there's more than one kind of shark in these parts,' he added, glaring at Neville.

'Oh, this is heaps better than my plot,' I said, admiringly.

'Naturally – it's a soap, not a computer programme!' Jake explained.

I stared. 'You knew it wouldn't turn out like I planned! But you let me get all that equipment just the same.'

'Of course,' said Jake. 'This way Calvin isn't just a star roller-blader, he's a hero. Using his expensive new blades to fight the shark was a brilliant twist. I told you, magic is like music. You wrote a good song, okay? But Calvin had to sing it *his* way. Now watch. This is his big moment!'

Calvin came jetting across the centre runway and went into his routine. And let me tell you, he didn't just beat Neville. He *mashed* him like potatoes. He came out of the final electrifying stunt to deafening applause. Then he just stood there, scowling shyly at everyone as if he didn't know what to do next.

Suddenly Karen threw her arms round his neck. 'I love you, Calvin,' she cried.

'But I've always loved *you*,' he said astonished.

'Happy now, Lizzy?' Jake murmured in my ear.

The man from Blade City was murmuring poetry into his mobile. 'The boy defied gravity like a fallen angel,' he burbled. 'I want the press down here, I want the TV cameras ...'

Jake and I left him and Calvin in the park, talking business.

As it was, I only just caught the last post. I got a bit carried away in the post office, writing a letter to put in with the pen. I felt I owed Harvey Spangler the truth somehow.

I'd always meant to send it back anyway. I mean I knew it couldn't go on for ever. But when the postman went off with Harvey Spangler's pen in his sack, that old, empty feeling came over me again. I could feel my whole life shrinking, like a sweater I'd grown out of. Jake saw my face.

'It's not over yet, Cinders,' he teased, 'you've still got till midnight.'

We found a little restaurant with a perfect
view of the sun setting over the bay.

Then after our meal, we went off to the rest-rooms to change into our amazing new glad-rags. But when we finally set out through rich tropical darkness, I started to shake with terror. 'Jake,' I said, 'I think I've changed my mind.'

'No way,' said Jake. 'Calvin's had his moment: this is yours.'

'Jake, how is that the same? Calvin's a roller-blade wizard. But this isn't me at all. It's a dream. Just a stupid dream. Tomorrow I'll be back in the real Greybridge. All I'll have left from today is memories. I want them to be good ones.' My eyes filled with tears.

To my relief the cafe was dark and silent. The party had obviously been cancelled at the last minute.

But as we reached the door, lights sprang on everywhere. 'Surprise surprise!' people yelled inside. 'Happy birthday, Angie.'

'Where did you rogues come from!' we heard Angie cry, happily.

'I can't do this, Jake!' I said in a low voice.

'I'm going home.' I started to walk away.

'Wait!' said Jake. He grabbed my hand and hung on to it. 'You know the great thing about soaps? Scriptwriters rewrite characters all the time and no one minds a bit. But in real life you can get stuck being the person everyone else *thinks* you are.'

'Yes,' I said, amazed he understood. 'It's like no one sees the real you. Like you're trapped inside a disguise. But inside, there's all these invisible dreams.'

'You did more than dream today,' said Jake. 'You rewrote the character of Lizzy Lemon. *You* did that, Lizzy – not me, not the pen. You set her free to do everything she ever dreamed of. But if you really want to be a star,' he said fiercely, 'you'd better get in there now and *sparkle*!'

I stared at him. I wasn't sure, but I thought Jake had just told me *I* was magic.

That couldn't be true, could it? But while I was puzzling over this, Jake pushed me firmly into the cafe ahead of him.

'Glad you kids could make it,' beamed Angie. 'Ooh, pressies too!' she gloated, as Jake and I handed her our presents.

'Lizzy's keeping the best present for later,' said Jake, wickedly.

Calvin loped up with a grin wider than a Halloween pumpkin. 'Lizzy, can you believe it – that Blade City dude signed me up?! If I play my cards right, I'll earn enough money from roller-blading to go to college after all.'

'That's brilliant, Calvin,' I said. 'I know you'll make it.' I gave him a shy hug. For a minute I was so happy for him, I forgot how scared I was about the surprise present we'd planned for Angie.

That wasn't all I forgot. I also forgot the soap rule that says, no beautiful moment lasts longer than a few heartbeats and what comes next is always incredibly dark.

'Hiya, babe,' said a familiar voice. And suddenly, there was Karen in a tight, red dress the spit of Kelly's, clinging to Calvin's arm. 'Well, haven't you been busy, Lizzy!'

Karen was smiling her foxy Scarlet smile, but the look in her eyes was pure poison. 'A real Miss Fixit,' she spat out. 'But as your best friend I've got to tell you – that new hairstyle is a big mistake. As for the dress – Lizzy, honestly! Look, you've got your own sweet funny style, babe. You don't have to impress us. We love you just the way you are.'

A stunned silence fell on everyone. And though I didn't see anyone actually move, the party kind of melted to the edges of the cafe. Now Karen and I were left alone in the middle, face to face, like gunfighters in an old western. And I got the weirdest sensation, like I'd always known this was going to happen.

I couldn't believe she'd said those awful things. It wasn't like she wanted to hurt me, so much as rub me out altogether, like some stupid mistake everyone was laughing at. Well, I was hurt all right, but there was another feeling swirling around inside me too – a frighteningly new one. To give myself time to get used to it, I said, shakily, 'So, er – what's my own sweet, funny style then, Karen?'

Karen burst into peals of Scarletish laughter. 'It's obvious, babe. You're quiet and romantic and sweet and shy. You're a background person, Lizzy, and you always will be. Some people are just made that way.'

'I see,' I said. And I was amazed how calm I sounded. 'Well, thanks for clearing that up.'

Karen blinked. 'Lizzy, you should be careful, you know,' she said, huffily, 'you're getting a real attitude.'

'Good,' I said, 'it's about time.' The new feeling was coming to the boil, like lava bursting to get out of a volcano. I could taste it. It was white-hot and completely unstoppable and suddenly I knew what it was. It was rage. And I'm telling you – it felt *wonderful!*

'Karen,' I said, in a voice so strong I almost shocked myself, 'you can't take in what I'm saying now, but I'm going to say it just the same. I always knew we should send Harvey Spangler's pen back but I hung on to it. First, because I was a wimp and second, to help Calvin, because I so wanted you to be happy. But Karen, every single one of your dreams came true today. And look at you! You're about as happy as – as one of those cold-blooded man-eaters out in the bay.'

I took a deep breath. Being angry makes you surprisingly dizzy.

'How do I know?' I went on. 'Because you're putting me down, the same way you always do. And why? Because you can't bear anyone else to have any glory. I'm not blaming you,' and I imitated Karen's voice.

'It's "what you're like". It's your style. And you know what's so interesting about this whole business? Whether you're being my Karen or Scarlet or your own flipping spiteful twin, you're always exactly the same person – vain, selfish and incredibly mean! So when tomorrow comes and Greybridge goes back to normal, I won't be hanging round with you any more, okay? Because from now on, I'm writing my own story. And you know what, Karen? You're not even in it!'

Anger's a funny thing. As I walked away, I was bubbling with more energy than I've ever had in my life. So much that I had to do something with it there and then – something to prove the new Lizzy was here to stay.

Jake sat at the piano and pushed back his sleeves. 'Ready, Lizzy?' he said, quietly.

Was I? Actually, I wasn't sure I'd ever exactly be *ready*. But what's happening? Who's this in an outrageous dress, bounding on stage to join the band? Is it really me, sweet, shy Lizzy Lemon?

I grabbed the mike: 'This is specially for Angie. It's called *Soft Soap*.' And as Jake crashed out the first honky tonk chords, I shook out my spiky new hair and I started to belt it out like Tina Turner. And it wasn't one of Havana's songs. It was mine.

The last line went:

'Never order a knickerbocker glory if you don't want your wicked twin to spoil the story!'

As the notes died away, everyone stamped and hooted. Calvin whistled through his fingers. But my ex-best friend Karen was nowhere to be seen.

'You fraud,' chuckled Angie. 'Under those ugly duckling clothes, you were a wild rock chick all the time! So will you jump on this, Lizzy, or shall I? It's obvious you don't want it, or you wouldn't keep leaving it behind.' And she held out Havana's romantic, daisy hat.

'Tell you what ...' I grinned, 'let's take it in turns.'

I don't remember much about the rest of the evening, but all at once I was with Jake in the taxi and it was time to say goodbye. We'd said all the important things already, but I still didn't want to let him go.

'Where will you go?' I asked, huskily.

'On to the next story,' he said, 'same as you. But from now on, Lizzy Lemon, I'll be betting all your stories will have a little sparkle of star-dust in them.'

The taxi slowed down and I got out. I had a real shock when I saw what had happened to our house since yesterday. To be fair, people had been talking about it all day. I just hadn't taken it in.

The taxi slid away into the tropical night. I swallowed hard – I was going to miss Jake Cutter.

But by my calculations I only had half an hour left before Greybridge recovered from the soap spell and my parents came back. So I opened our front door and went up to my bedroom. It took for ever, climbing up all those twisting flights of stairs, and I made the most of every one.

Because, for the first and last time in my life, I was going to be sleeping in a windmill.

About the author

Everyone knows TV soaps are silly, but somehow we keep watching them.

During one long winter term at my school, another girl and I made up our own soap in which we also starred. This memory was the starting point for *Paradise High*.

Writing this story was sheer fun from start to finish, like going on a wonderful holiday with my characters! Lizzy, my heroine, is a bit like I was when I was growing up. On the outside, she seems easy to push around, but inside she's dying for an excuse to break out and be wild and outrageous!